SIMPLE COUNTRY
FURNITURE
PROJECTS

SCALE

D1088773

DEMCO

SIMPLE COUNTRY
FURNITURE
PROJECTS

IN 1/12 SCALE

Alison J White

GUILD OF MASTER
CRAFTSMAN PUBLICATIONS LTD

First published 2003 by
Guild of Master Craftsman Publications Ltd,
166 High Street, Lewes,
East Sussex BN7 1XU

Text copyright © Alison J White
Copyright in the Work © Guild of Master Craftsman Publications Ltd

ISBN 1 86108 351 3
A catalogue record of this book is available from the British Library.

Publisher: Paul Richardson
Art Director: Ian Smith
Production Manager: Stuart Poole
Managing Editor: Gerrie Purcell
Editor: James Evans

Cover and book design: Wheelhouse Design
Typeface: Garamond and Optima

Photographs: Anthony Bailey
except those on pages viii and 3 © Hulton Archive
Illustrations: Wheelhouse Design
based on originals by Penny Brown

Colour origination: P.T Repro Multi Warna
Printed and bound: Kyodo Singapore

I would like to thank April and James at GMC for all their help and guidance
with the preparation for this book.

For the very special people in my life – Perry, Sheila and Pat.

CONTENTS

An Irish couple at home in their cottage on the Aran Islands in County Galway.

INTRODUCTION

I became interested in antique country furniture when I moved to Northern Ireland in 1980. The limited interest in the subject at that time meant it was possible to collect pieces easily and quite cheaply. There was usually a story attached to individual items and sometimes, if I was lucky, information about where they had come from and the uses that had been made of them. Rather than the kind of furniture that would have been found in big houses, antique country furniture is the sort of everyday item that would have been affordable to the greater number of families. As such, it gives an insight into the social history of times both within living memory and long ago.

Rarely mass-produced, this type of furniture was made either by the householder, a local craftsman or a journeyman (a travelling carpenter who worked in exchange for some food and a bed for the night). More often than not, country furniture was made to fit a specific place in the house or cottage and was, therefore, hardly ever produced in sufficient numbers to ensure matching sets. Pieces were generally made using whatever materials were available, which might have meant recycling. Sections of cartwheels could be used for the rockers on a cradle, for example, and wood washed up on the shore was also useful.

This one-off nature ensures uniqueness, but also suitability for the job required. Each piece would have had to be practical and may have had multiple uses. For example, a settle bed often doubled as both a day seat, an extra bed and sometimes even a playpen for a child. Many children may well have learned to walk within the safe confines of a settle, with a convenient side to hold on to. Even a single chair, laid on its back, would have been used as a 'parking' place for a small child.

Despite their ad hoc construction, country furniture items are now becoming increasingly collectable and are eminently suitable for either a town house or a country cottage, blending equally well with modern or period decor. Indeed, many of the projects featured in this book are based on pieces of furniture from my own home. These would have been in regular use throughout Great Britain and Ireland, but similar histories of vernacular furniture can be found in Switzerland, Germany, the Scandinavian countries and many Eastern European countries, as well as in the well-known style of Shaker furniture found in the United States.

It is frequently possible to ascribe some pieces to their country of origin due to the various styles employed by the journeymen at the time. An example of this is the Irish table, which usually has a double stretcher underneath. Wales is synonymous with dressers, while items commonly found in the south of England include chests of drawers and tall kitchen dressers. Scotland is famous for large chests of drawers.

Country furniture was frequently made of a mixture of pine, oak, ash, beech or other locally grown wood. Inevitably this suffered considerable damage over the years from woodworm and damp. As a consequence, the practice of using 'boot' or 'sledge' feet to counteract the damp was introduced. As soon as the feet started to rot away they were replaced with new ones, prolonging the life of the item of furniture. Many pieces have been repaired in this way, as it was necessary to replace the legs of chairs, beds and other items that had become damp on beaten-earth floors or worn on hard flagstones.

While today the fashion is to strip furniture back to bare wood, in its original state it would have been painted, often with several coats of paint one on top of another obscuring some of the decorative work. In Ireland, for instance, a home would have been given a spring clean and its furniture a fresh coat of paint whenever the householder was preparing to play host, such as when a priest came to administer mass.

Knife grinders at work outside a rustic English cottage.

PART ONE

Before you begin

Examples of different finishes.

METHODS

The aim in developing this book was to make the instructions as simple as possible, bearing in mind that most miniaturists (like the author) are not joiners or woodturners and have only limited woodworking skills, but nevertheless are happy to turn their hand to DIY in 1/12 scale. The projects are set out in order, with the easier projects first, so that anyone who works right through to the end will gain confidence in their abilities, and sufficient pieces of furniture to form the basis of a small cottage. Some projects use similar techniques, or form part of another piece. For instance, the top section of the dresser is based on the wall-mounted cupboard.

The pieces can be stained, painted, or varnished and waxed to give them the same lovely warm patina as their full-size relatives. Wood stain or a quick-drying wood varnish will allow the grain on the wood to remain visible, while painting with diluted coffee or tea can age untreated pieces. In this book most of the projects are left untreated, leaving the reader to finish them in a way that is appropriate to their own setting. Larger pieces of furniture, in a cottage-type setting, would undoubtedly be painted in fairly basic colours such as brown, cream, blue, or red. If the furniture is placed in a modern house it would be stained and waxed, thus retaining the natural, aged look of the antique cottage style.

Left, you can see two possible treatments. The wall-mounted cupboard has been stained and then had two layers of varnish applied (lightly sanded between coats), before being finished with wax polish. The chair has been given two different coats of paint, and the second coat sanded in places to give the appearance of wear. At intervals throughout the instructions for each project you will notice that I suggest light sanding. I cannot emphasise enough the importance of sanding lightly, as vigorous use of sandpaper can alter the shape of wood with surprising speed.

Look closely at the wood that you are planning to use, and downsize the grain of the wood in your own mind to check for authenticity. Personally, I prefer not to use either the very soft or more open-grained woods, but there are no hard-and-fast rules – go for the look that suits you.

While at the planning stage, think about the context of the furniture. Has the piece been made lovingly for a specific place in a house? If so, was it made in a very simple style with square wooden legs, or was it made with turned legs to look more decorative? The latter effect can be achieved easily by using ready-made spindles or chunkier newel posts, both of which can be cut to the desired size.

Another tip worth remembering is that the size of furniture today is larger than that in general use in previous centuries because people were not as tall. Also, space was at a premium within buildings – with no central heating it was more practical to keep the living and sleeping space small enough to conserve heat. I found this out for myself after purchasing a bed frame that is over a hundred years old from a specialist in cottage antiques. The only way to get a mattress to fit was to have one made specially by a mattress company that recognised the measurements as those of an antique Irish bed.

All measurements are given in inches first, with the approximate metric equivalent (given in millimetres) shown in brackets. I recommend that you decide whether you are going to use the imperial or metric measurement at an early stage, and then stick to that. Otherwise there may be discrepancies in the sizes. I have made additional suggestions for making pieces bigger or smaller as required. Even so, it can be difficult for the hobbyist to keep measurements and cutting accurate (no matter how hard I try things frequently fail to fit together perfectly – thank goodness for sandpaper), but mistakes are not the end of the world. After all, in the full-scale versions, marks and wear are seen as part of the patina that has come with use.

One way to help avoiding mistakes is to use a very fine pencil, ideally one with a retractable lead that is no more than 0.5mm thick. These are widely available in stationery shops. Any pencil marks that are still on the wood after construction can be removed with a soft eraser, provided that the lines are lightly drawn.

Occasionally, however hard you try to keep to scale, the piece just doesn't look right. A very useful exercise is to take photographs of rooms or individual pieces of furniture. That way it is possible to see through the eyes of a camera, and to show your work to other people.

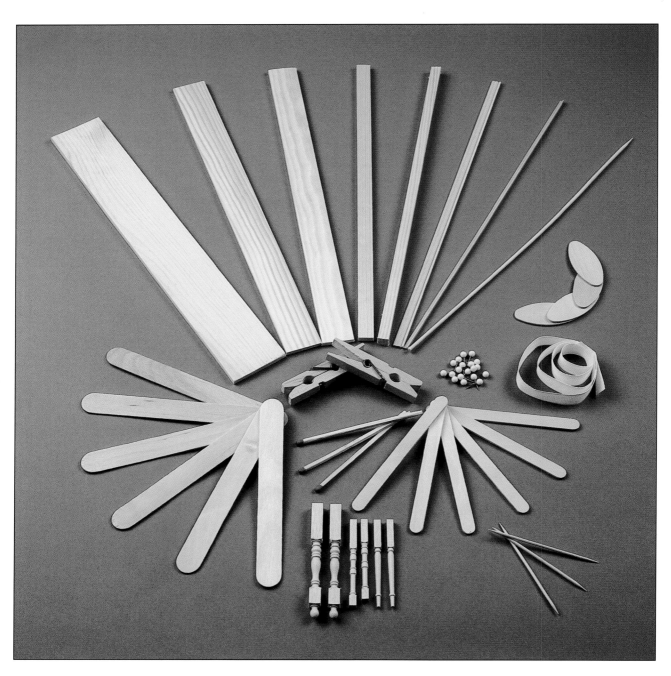

Some of the materials used to make the projects in this book.

MATERIALS

To help the hobbyist, the materials used here are readily available from DIY stores or hobby shops. Some specialist wood supplies are available through mail-order companies and mouldings can be purchased from many dolls' house suppliers. The wood used is mostly strip wood from chain DIY shops, but there are some machine-tooled mouldings, such as architrave and spindles, from a specialist supplier (see page 89 for details of specialist suppliers). The strip wood is very well finished and comes with at least two of its sides machined already so that they are parallel (leaving less room for mistakes). Ice-lolly or craft sticks are available in several sizes and shapes, and it is worth keeping a stock of them. Should the miniaturist not have access to a ready supply of strip wood, it would be equally possible to make the pieces using good-quality birch plywood. Other sources of wood are matches; the long ones make excellent bars for the backs of chairs. Cocktail sticks and kebab sticks are also extremely useful for the miniaturist as a source of ready-turned wood. I have even been known to collect any kebab sticks left after a working lunch and take them home to be washed and recycled!

The choice of glue is important. Clear-drying PVA tacky glue is good because if, despite your best efforts, a tiny amount escapes, it won't show. However, it should be water-soluble so that any excess can be wiped off with a damp cloth before it dries. Glue left on the piece prevents wood taking up any wood stain, although it will take a coat of paint or varnish without any bother. Should you have shaky hands it is probably better to stain the wood before gluing it. If the container does not come with a fine applicator or nib, spills can be avoided by applying the glue with a cocktail stick.

Superglue will give you an instant result, but in time it will deteriorate and need reapplication. If the effect of an instant 'grab' would be useful, and you have the space, a solution is to use a tiny blob of superglue and put PVA glue alongside it. The gel form of superglue is easier to place and is less likely to run.

Many hobby or dolls' house suppliers offer ready-made architraves, coving and spindles should the idea of making your own be a bit off-putting. (I am quite happy to use other people's work in this way – routing is not something that I can cope with.) These professionally manufactured pieces will finish off some of the furniture and make an enormous difference to the end result.

I have not used ready-made hinges in any of these projects, but make my own using cotton tape, which takes glue well and can be coloured with varnish or paint. Affixing ready-made hinges takes an enormous amount of patience and time, but there is no reason, if you have the skill, why they should not be used wherever I have used a cloth hinge.

A selection of tools helpful to miniaturists.

USEFUL TOOLS

- Mitre block suitable for miniature work
- Small hacksaw or razor saw
- Gluing board (see page 14)
- Various small clamps (some pet stores sell tiny plastic clamps that are intended for altering the flow through piping in a fish tank, and these can be very useful when you are working on a small piece)
- Vice or 'helping hands' tool
- Sticky tape (which is also useful for holding pieces together until the glue has dried)
- Fine sandpaper
- Set of needle files (very useful for shaping)
- Hobby drill
- Metal safety ruler
- Pencil (preferably one with a retractable 0.5mm tip)
- Tracing paper
- Try square (a miniature one is best, or alternatively a set square from a geometry set)
- Match cutter
- Self-healing cutting mat
- Craft knife
- Scissors
- Wire cutters
- PVA tacky glue
- Superglue (preferably in gel form)
- An old piece of white candle
- Tin can (an unopened one is great for weighing down projects while they dry)

MAKING A GLUING BOARD

A gluing board is invaluable for ensuring that sides or legs are at right angles to bases and tops. However much you are longing to get on with the projects, time and care spent in making the board will reward you with a useful piece of equipment.

Method

- Take a piece of medium-density fibreboard (MDF) or plywood (if ply is being used, it is important to find a piece that is thick enough not to warp) big enough for the finished board to be approximately 8in (20cm) by 6in (15cm).

- To ensure that the completed board has perfect right angles, first draw a straight line with a ruler and fine pencil, and saw carefully along it. Then, using a try square, draw a line at right angles to the cut edge. If you are using a miniaturist's tool, extend the line to the required length with a ruler, and carefully cut the second edge.

Parts for the gluing board.

The completed gluing board. Clingfilm ensures that your work doesn't stick the surface.

- Continue to measure and cut the angles with care, making sure that opposite sides are of the same length. You should now have a neat piece of wood that is a perfect square or rectangle.

- Measure and cut a piece of wood approximately 1½in (38mm) by ½in (13mm) to exactly the same length as one of the sides. The use of a mitre block at this stage will ensure that the wood is cut at right angles to the long edge. Smooth down the cut edges by sanding them lightly.

- Using PVA glue, stick the narrow edge of the wood to the matching edge of the board, then leave the board long enough to ensure that the baton is well stuck down to its matching edge.

- Once the first side is firmly stuck in place, measure and cut a piece of wood for the second side.

- Glue both the long edge and the end of the baton before carefully gluing this at right angles to the first side. Use a try square at this point to ensure a perfect angle.

- Leave the board until the glue is set, so that there is no possibility of the sides moving.

- If you want to make sure that the gluing board will retain its angles, you could hammer three or four small pins or nails through the base so that they go into the sides.

- Your gluing board is now ready for use, but first cover it with a sheet of clingfilm (see Glossary, page 86). This is so thin that it will not interfere with your measurements, and it will ensure that nothing becomes stuck to the board.

WORKING SAFETY

- Make sure that sharp tools are kept sharp. Using craft knives with a snap-off blade will help to ensure that you always have a sharp blade to work with. Blades that are blunt are more likely to slip, but are still sharp enough to cut fingers. Don't use sharp blades or hobby drills when there is a child or pet in the room.

- The projects might be miniature, but the dust can still be hazardous. Make sure that there is plenty of ventilation and wear a mask if the job is going to be dusty. The dust from MDF is thought to be particularly hazardous. A well-ventilated area is also necessary when using glue or paint.

- Keep a clean and tidy working area. I'm not a fanatic when it comes to housework, but you will find it easier and safer if your working space is clear.

- Consider buying a gardener's potting tray. The raised sides will help to keep all your working tools in a manageable space that can be moved out of reach halfway through the project – away from small fingers and pets.

- Nearly everything that you will be using or making could choke a small child. Store the bits and pieces that you are keeping for future use in boxes that are childproof.

- When cutting a straight line with a craft knife use a metal ruler or, even better, a metal safety ruler that keeps your fingers away from the blade. Work on a self-healing cutting mat to help prevent the work from slipping.

- Any tool that is sharp or pointed should have a cover. If this has gone missing use a cork or a segment cut from an eraser.

- Using a daylight-simulating bulb will reduce the strain on your eyes when working in artificial light.

Storage and care of materials

- Wood, even strip wood, can warp very easily. Try to store it at room temperature, and keep it as flat as possible.

- Paint and glue containers are best stored upright and at room temperature. A plastic tray with raised sides is ideal for this purpose.

- Self-healing cutting mats will warp if they are stored on end. The best way to ensure that they remain as flat as possible is to leave them in position on a flat working surface.

- Glue can very easily clog up the 'nib' of its container. A glass-headed pin kept in the nib makes it easier to keep the hole clear.

- Manufacturers of superglue usually make a removing fluid for dealing with things that have accidentally got stuck together. Keep a bottle handy – not only will it unglue fingers, it will help to keep the superglue container itself clean.

QUICK TIPS

Quick tip 1

White, round-headed map tacks can be used to simulate Victorian-style china handles very effectively. First, find the centre of your drawer by lightly drawing both diagonals with a pencil to find out where they cross. Use the map tack to make a hole for the handle where the lines cross, but do not push it all the way in. Use wire cutters to reduce the pin to half its size (being careful to watch where the discarded section of the pin goes, as it tends to fly off). With a little bit of glue on the tack shank, push the cut-down version into the drawer front (first rubbing out the pencil lines). Try to avoid using a hammer for this, as the head of the tack tends to split. Painted with coloured varnish, the handles can also be made to look wooden.

Quick tip 2

Sometimes, no matter how hard you try, small slivers of wood can remain after using a saw. Rather than trying to eliminate them with sandpaper straight away, cut them off with a pair of scissors, and then smooth the edges with sandpaper.

Quick tip 3

Wood stain does exactly that: it stains – everything! Try using a cotton-wool bud to apply the stain. It reaches into small recesses, keeps the wood stain off your fingers, and can be discarded when finished with. You may need to use more than one on each piece, as rough treatment will cause the bud to start to fray and leave minute threads on your work.

Quick tip 4

PVA glue can be used to fill gaps if your measurements did not turn out to be as accurate as you had intended. The only problem is that it will not take up stain. However, a coloured varnish will still give a good finish.

Quick tip 5

When using sandpaper always sand in the direction of the grain. Sanding across the grain will leave marks on the surface that will take a huge amount of work to eradicate, and this may spoil the appearance of the finished piece.

Quick tip 6

Should your saw blade start to stick, take a piece of a white candle and rub it on the blade of the saw. Any residue left on the wood that you are cutting can be removed with sandpaper.

PART TWO

The projects

PROJECT 1

Dough-kneading board

A dough-kneading board is a useful item that would have been found in most houses, whatever the social standing of the occupants. Bread has always been an important part of the diet and bread making would have been a daily household activity. The flour used to make it was too precious to waste, so the thrifty housewife used a board with three raised sides to ensure that none of the flour was spilt when kneading the dough. Many regions produced their own speciality breads – such as bannock, potato bread, farls, lava bread and cottage loaves – depending on the type of flour and other ingredients that were available in the area. The dough-kneading board does not need a coat of paint or a varnished finish, as the full-size version would have been regularly scrubbed clean with sand or salt and water.

This is a simple project, but you will find that the technique will be used as part of several, more complex projects later in the book. There are no hard-and-fast rules regarding the size of the base of the dough-kneading board; it would depend on the size of the household and the table it was to sit on.

PROJECT 1

Method

- Saw a piece of strip wood approximately 1⅜in (35mm) by 2in (50mm) to form the base of the board, and then sand the edges smooth.

- Measure one of the long edges and cut a section of craft stick to the same length (avoiding the rounded ends), then lightly sand the cut ends.

- Glue the piece of craft stick to the back of the long edge of the dough-kneading board, using the gluing board to ensure that it is at right angles to the base. (The craft-stick pieces will, in effect, be 'wrapped' around 3 sides of the body of the dough-kneading board.)

- Once the glue has dried, measure the short edges of the dough-kneading board (remembering to include the raised back of craft stick that you have already glued to the base) and cut two identical side pieces, also from craft stick.

- Using fine-grade sandpaper, lightly sand one end of each side section. In this way, round off one of the corners, as shown in the exploded view.

- Glue the two sides to the dough-kneading board one at a time, once again using the gluing board to ensure a right-angled join.

- Leave to dry, preferably overnight. If you are too impatient for this, you will find many types of glue that dry in about 20 minutes – just make sure that you don't put too much pressure on any of the raised edges until the glue is up to full strength.

PROJECT 2

Candle box

Candles were commonplace in many houses right up until the early part of the twentieth century. They had to be kept dry, so a candle box was often hung on the wall near the fireplace. The late nineteenth century saw the introduction of gas as a light source, and as a source of heat for cooking. In the country and in less affluent houses, however, candles and hand-held oil lamps were still used routinely. In rural areas, some houses were without electricity until the 1950s.

The candle box is another relatively simple piece, but with the additional option of decorating it with a small trefoil should you want to (see page 84 for a template of possible decorations). Also, lengths can be cut from a wax taper and the ends shaped using a craft knife to look like candles.

PROJECT 2

Tools

- Hacksaw or razor saw
- Mitre block
- Sandpaper
- Gluing board
- Metal ruler
- Fine pencil
- Hobby drill
- Craft knife
- Needle files

Method

- Take a large craft stick (or tongue depressor), measure and cut off approximately 1¾in (45mm), including the rounded end, using a mitre block and hacksaw, and then lightly sand the sawn edge. This will be the back of your box.

- At this stage you need to decide if the candle box is to be completely plain or to have some decoration. A simple, common decoration is a trefoil or clover pattern. This can be achieved quite simply by marking a light line down the centre of the back with a pencil and then measuring a spot ¼in (6mm) below the rounded edge. Tape the back to a

CANDLE BOX

spare piece of thicker wood and, with the piece secured firmly in a vice, drill a hole through this spot using a drill bit between $\frac{3}{32}$ and $\frac{2}{16}$in (2.3 and 3.2mm) in size. Make sure that the hole goes right through the back, and then carefully make two more holes to complete the decoration, as shown in the exploded view (left). Remember: craft sticks are very thin, so the support must be left in place until the three holes have been made. Trim off any excess wood within the trefoil with a sharp craft knife, or use a needle file to smooth and enlarge the holes as necessary. Finally, using an eraser, remove any remaining pencil marks.

- To complete the box, cut three identical pieces $\frac{3}{4}$in (20mm) in length from the remaining piece of craft stick, measuring from the cut end. Then lightly sand the sawn edges. These will form the other two sides and the front of the box.

- Place the candle box on its back on the gluing board, with the side edge against one side wall. Glue the edge of one of the side pieces and set it at right angles to the back, ensuring that it is held firmly in place until dry.

- Repeat this with the second side piece.

- The front of the candle box will now fit in place across the two sides, and should be glued in position. Use sticky tape to hold the box together while it is drying, if necessary.

- The base of the box needs to be measured fairly accurately to give a good finish, and there are two options for doing this. The easiest way is to stand the box on the remaining piece of craft stick and, with a very fine pencil, draw lightly around the outside edges. The other way is to stand the box on the craft stick and, again using a very fine pencil, draw around the inside of the box's base.

- The wood should then be cut to size, and either the bottom edges of the box or the edges of the base piece (depending on the way you measured and cut it) glued.

- Finally, put the base in place carefully, and allow the glue to dry before sanding any remaining rough edges.

- The completed candle box can then be painted, stained, varnished or waxed.

Materials

- Large craft sticks or tongue depressors
- PVA glue

PROJECT 3

Knife box

Surprising though it may seem, the knife box was not for holding knives. In fact, it would have been filled with sand or a stone and used for keeping knives clean and sharp. The long back to the box was part of the sharpening process, and if sand was used, the back acted in much the same way as a barber's leather strop.

The instructions for making this piece of household equipment are very similar to those for the candle box, the main difference being that it is a thinner box with a longer back piece. This model has quite a long back, but it could be made shorter if required.

Tools

- Hacksaw or razor saw
- Mitre block
- Sandpaper
- Gluing board
- Metal ruler
- Fine pencil
- Hobby drill
- Craft knife
- Needle files

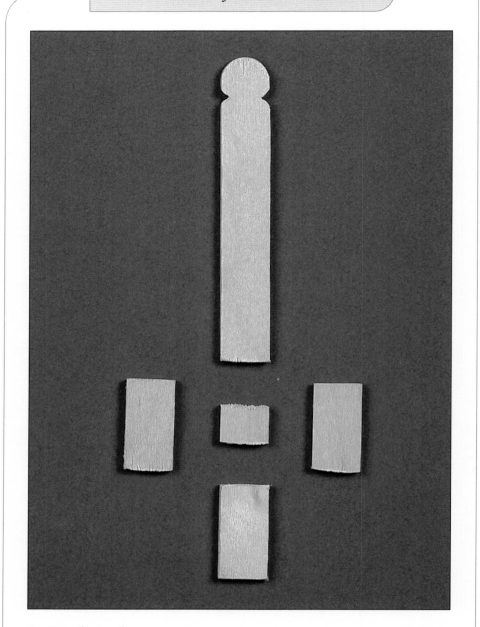

Method

- Take a small craft stick, measure and cut off approximately 2⅜ inches (60mm) including the rounded end, using a mitre block and hacksaw, and lightly sand the sawn edge. This will be the long back of your box.

- You must now decide if your knife box is to be completely plain, or if it is to have some

KNIFE BOX

decoration. Simple decoration can be achieved by cutting two notches, one on either side of the back piece. As shown in the exploded view, these have been cut, using a sharp craft knife, approximately ¼in (6mm) below the rounded edge.

- To add to further decoration you can use a hobby drill to cut a small circle, as shown in the photo of the completed knife box. Trim off any excess wood with a sharp craft knife, or use a needle file to smooth and enlarge the decoration as necessary.

- To complete the box, cut three identical pieces of craft stick ¾ in (20mm) in length, and lightly sand the sawn edges. These pieces will be used to form the other three sides.

- Lay the back of the knife box on the surface of the gluing board, with the side edge pressed against one side wall. Glue the edge of one of the side pieces at right angles to the back, and ensure that it is held firmly in place until well dried.

- Repeat with a second side piece, leaving enough time between the two for the glue to dry – there is nothing more frustrating than moving on too quickly, only to find that the previous stage has become loose.

- The front of the knife box will now fit in place across the two sides, and should be glued in position. Use sticky tape to hold the box together while it is drying, if necessary.

- The base of the box needs to be measured fairly accurately to give a good finish and, as with the candle box, there are two options for doing this. The easiest way is to stand the box on the remaining piece of craft stick and, with a very fine pencil, draw lightly around the outside edges. Alternatively, stand the box on the craft stick and, again using a very fine pencil, draw around the inside of the box's base.

- The wood should then be cut to the relevant size, and either the bottom edges of the box or the edges of the base piece (depending on the way you measured and cut it) glued.

- Finally, carefully put the base in place, and allow the glue to dry before sanding any remaining rough edges.

- The completed knife box can then be painted, stained, varnished or waxed. If you are planning to use it in a period cottage, the finish should look like darkened wood, caused by its proximity to an open fire.

Materials

- Two small craft (or ice-lolly) sticks
- PVA glue

PROJECT 4

Stool/bench

In the past, most dwelling places would have used stools or benches as a form of seating. Many households may also have had a pair of stools of equal height called 'coffin' stools, upon which coffins were set while the family held a wake for the deceased.

Stools were easy to make as the family increased in number, and would have been built very simply. One version, sometimes known as a 'creepie', was just a block of wood with four very short legs. The version shown here is a bit more elaborate, with sides and a small hole in the top for easy lifting.

Older or sick members of the family were placed near to the fire in a sturdier chair that had arms and a back. As cooking and warmth came from the same fireplace, this ensured that not only was this family member nearest to the source of heat, they were also cared for in the heart of the family. At meal times, the adults might have been seated on a settle, and a bench or stools pulled up to the table for the younger members of the family.

This project can be made either as a long bench or a short stool, and can be any size that seems appropriate for the space available. I have several full-size stools ranging in size from 10in (25cm) high and 12in (30cm) long, to one that is 14in (36cm) high and 18in (46cm) long.

You will need to decide whether your miniature is for a period setting or a modern one, as central heating dries out wooden furniture. This can cause the original wedge-and-pegged tenon joints to rise. Don't panic – I am not suggesting that the joints have to be pegged, but it is possible to fake the joints in an authentic-looking way.

PROJECT 4

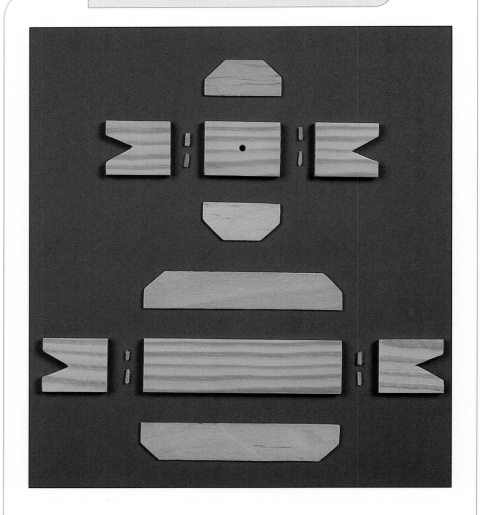

Method

■ Cut a length of 1⅛in (28mm) wide strip wood to form the top of the stool. The exact length will depend on the room setting and the space that is available, but if you are unsure cut a piece 1½in (38mm) long.

■ If the stool is to be as authentic as possible, hold the top firmly in a clamp and drill a small hole in the centre to act as a finger hole. (The exact centre can be found by lightly drawing a line across each of the diagonals.) To simulate the wear from years of lifting up the stool, use a needle file to alter the shape of the hole slightly.

■ From the same piece of strip wood, cut two pieces that are identical in size to each other.

STOOL/BENCH

These will form the legs of the stool, and should be about 1¼in (32mm) in length.

- Mark a V-shaped notch in the leg pieces, as in the exploded diagram, to form the legs. (The two pieces could be taped together first to ensure that the notches are the same.)

- Lightly sand all the cut edges.

- Turn the seat over and measure in from the short edge, to mark the position of the legs. I suggest a distance of approximately ¼in (6mm) from the edge.

- Glue the legs onto the underside of the stool and leave them to set.

- Carefully measure your stool and cut two pieces of craft stick the same length as the top of the seat.

- Shape the sides by sanding the corners slightly or sawing the angle of the corners away in the way shown in the exploded photograph (opposite).

- Placing the side level with the top of the stool, glue it into position. When this is dry, repeat with the other side panel.

- At this point, you need to make a decision about the joints. If you are going to add them, use a match cutter to cut four pieces from a matchstick and glue these on the top side of the stool above the position of the legs.

- Complete the stool in a finish of your choice.

If you want to make the bench, decide on the length that it will be and replace the measurements for the stool, cutting the top piece to this length. I suggest 4in (10cm).

Materials

- Large craft sticks or tongue depressors
- Strip wood
- PVA glue
- Matchsticks

PROJECT 5

Salt box

Salt has long been an important condiment in the kitchen. It has been used to flavour foods, as well as to cure and preserve items in times when there was no other way of making food last through the winter. In Ireland particularly, salt was a vital part of the diet. During the nineteenth century, the staple food was potatoes, to which might be added a little milk. In the absence of this, a helping of salt gave flavour. Another use for salt was as a cleaning agent; utensils that were made of wood, such as breadboards or tables, were frequently scrubbed with salt and water. Salt boxes, with their sloping lid, were hung near to the fire to keep their precious contents dry.

The method for making the salt box starts in much the same way as the candle box, but this project introduces the idea of using cotton tape as a hinge. I have suggested that, for this project, all the pieces of wood should be cut and sanded before beginning any gluing. You will need to measure quite carefully to ensure that all the pieces fit together, as the box has sloped sides and an opening lid. A note of warning here: the sections are relatively large to be using wood as fine as the large craft sticks, but the end result is easier to achieve this way. Had I used the thicker, stronger strip wood it would need chamfering to allow for the sloped sides. The completed box is sturdy enough, however, to fill with salt if you wish.

Tools

- Hacksaw or razor saw
- Mitre box
- Sandpaper
- Metal ruler
- Fine pencil
- Hobby drill
- Needle files

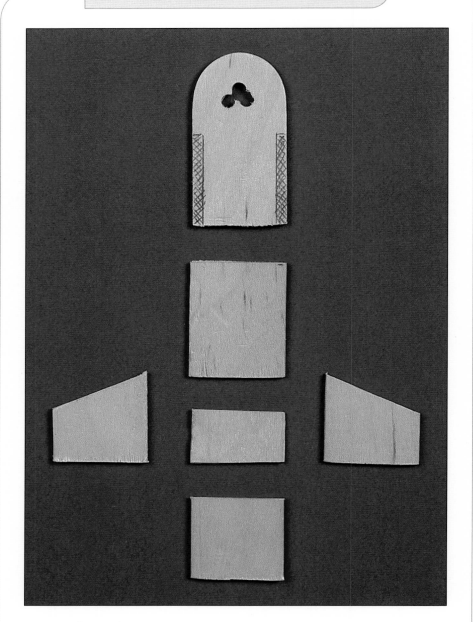

Method

- Take one of the large craft sticks, measure off approximately 1½in (38mm) including the rounded end, cut across the stick using a mitre block and hacksaw, then lightly sand the sawn edge. This will be the back of your box.

- At this stage, as with the candle box, you need to decide if the salt box is to be completely plain

SALT BOX

or have some decoration. The trefoil pattern can be repeated in the same way as the candle box or it can have a painted motif.

- Tape together two pieces of large craft stick and cut them just above one of the rounded ends to create the straight-edged bottom of the box sides.

- Measuring from the base of the side pieces, lightly mark a dot ¾in (20mm) along one edge. On the other edge measure and mark ½in (13mm) along. Join the two marks with a ruler and saw along this line. You cannot use a mitre box to guide the saw blade as its use is limited to 90° or 45° cuts, so make sure that the craft sticks are firmly held in a vice before attempting to cut the wood. Once finished, you will have two side pieces with sloping top edges.

- To make the front of the box, cut a ½in (13mm) piece from the craft stick.

- The next piece of the box to make is the lid. For this, cut a piece that is slightly longer than the length of the sloped top edge of the sides.

- Lightly sand the cut edges of the front, top and side pieces.

- Place the back of the salt box in the gluing board against one of the sides.

- Sparingly glue along the long

back edge of one of the side pieces, and place it against the back section in the area that has been marked on the exploded view, making sure that the join forms a right angle. Leave the two pieces alone until the glue has hardened, then repeat for the second side.

- Glue the front section to the front (i.e. shorter) edges of the side pieces, ensuring that all four corners of the box form neat right angles.

- Cut a final piece of craft stick to form the base, and glue this into position. As in the two earlier projects, this can be measured by drawing around either the outside or inside (to make a slightly neater finish) of the box.

- While the rest of the box is drying, cut a small piece of cotton tape slightly shorter than the width of the craft stick, then glue this onto one of the cut ends of the lid section. This will form the hinge, so make sure that a flap of material is left for attaching the lid to the back of the box.

- Once the box is dry, glue the hinge into position.

- Finish the box with stain, varnish or paint.

Materials

- Large craft sticks or tongue depressors
- Small piece of cotton tape
- PVA glue

PROJECT 6

Table

Awooden table formed the hub of the kitchen, and would have been used for both preparing and eating food. In order to keep it clean it would have been scrubbed daily with sand, salt, or in later years, with a bar of soap. The top would therefore always be bare and bleached as a result of this repeated washing.

In its simplest form it would have been made with planks of wood laid across trestles. In some cottages in Ireland it was simply a piece of board with four legs made 'earth-fast' (i.e. sunken into the beaten-earth floor). Tables, being quite large objects, were sometimes attached to the wall or incorporated into a settle using hinges, and would have been let down only when they were needed. Items of country furniture often had more than one role. Typically, Irish tables would have had square rather than turned legs and also two parallel stretchers placed quite close to the floor. As well as increasing the stability of the table this would have provided more storage space, where bowls of milk or cooking equipment could be kept off the floor. Thatch and turf roofs provided weatherproof shelter, but became a refuge for small animals and insects; placing pails of milk and other pots beneath the table would have helped to stop anything undesirable from falling into them. Tables have even been found with small holes cut out to hold eggs.

They would have been made both with and without drawers underneath the table top. A drawer in the side would point to the table being made to fit along a wall; otherwise drawers would have been placed in one or both ends.

PROJECT 6

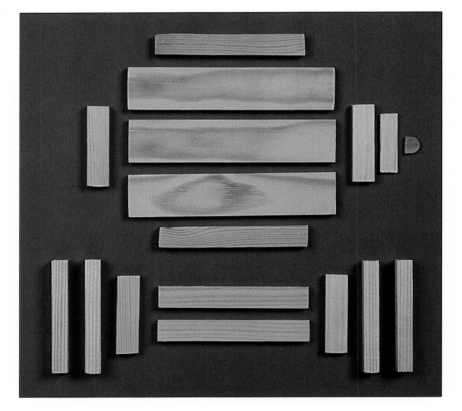

Tools

- Hacksaw or razor saw
- Mitre block
- Sandpaper
- Gluing board
- Metal ruler
- Fine pencil
- Try square

Method

- Using 1in (24mm) wide strip wood cut three pieces about 4½in (115mm) long (depending on the size of the room that the table is planned for). Make sure they are all the same length by using a steel rule, a very fine pencil and a try square.

- Place the first piece on the gluing board. Carefully glue one of the edges of another plank and stick it to the first piece. Repeat with the third plank and leave to dry. (A tin can is handy at this point to make sure that the three planks remain lying flat.)

- Having moved the tabletop to a safe place, cut four lengths of ⅜in square (10 x 10mm) strip wood, approximately 2½ inches (63mm) long. It is important that these are all exactly the same length or the table will wobble. If using spindles or upside-down newel posts you will need to decide on the height of the legs and cut off any excess.

- Using ½in (13mm) strip wood, cut two pieces 3¼in (80mm) and two pieces 1¾in (45mm). These will form the frame of the table and, together with the legs, will help to

TABLE

give the finished piece added strength and stability.

- Having lightly sanded any rough edges on the legs and frame, stand a table leg in the corner of the gluing board. If you are using a newel post this will be upside down (i.e. with the squared end pointing downwards).

- Glue one end of the longer frame piece to the leg, making sure that it is aligned with the side of the gluing board. Then stick one of the shorter frame pieces to the leg, but aligned with the other wall of the gluing board. Once the glue has dried, repeat with the remaining frame pieces, using a second leg.

- Still using the gluing board, place the other legs, one at a time, in the corner and complete the building of the support structure.

- Once it is dry and you have lightly sanded the cut ends, place the table top upside down, so that the underside is uppermost. Lift the support frame and legs (once they are dry) and place glue on the edges that will be stuck to the table. Gently place the legs and frame onto the table, leaving an even space around the edges to act as an overhang.

- You can leave the table at this stage, but it will be steadier and more realistic if stretchers and false drawers are added.

- Once the table is glued and dry, decide whether you will be placing it along a wall or in the centre of the room, and if it is to have drawers. (For this project the drawers are mock ones, although a later project gives instructions for making proper drawers).

- Using a small craft (or ice-lolly) stick, cut as many 1¼in (30mm) lengths as you want drawers. These can be placed individually on the ends or side-by-side on the longer side. Using some of the tiny rounded ends that you have cut off the craft sticks previously, you can make handles.

- From ½ in (13mm) strip wood, cut two pieces 1¾in (45mm) long. Lightly mark on one face of each leg the position that the cross pieces are to be, approximately ¼in (6mm) up from the base, and glue the shorter crosspieces in place. Measure the distance between the two short crosspieces and cut one or two stretchers to the same length. Slip the stretcher(s) in and glue them in position.

- Finish the table by staining, varnishing or painting the legs and frame. The table top should be left bare if you want to make it look like one that is cleaned with sand or salt and water.

Materials

- Strip wood
- Square strip wood (for the legs) or 4 spindles or newel posts, depending on the finished look that is required.
- Craft (or ice-lolly) sticks
- PVA glue

Washstand

This was an important item, especially in period houses where the plumbing was not up to the standards of the twenty-first century. Even in quite large houses there was often only one bathroom, so servants would have carried warm water to each bedroom twice a day. A disadvantage of this is that the water would have cooled quickly. The alternative was a tin bath in front of the fire, which would have been warmer, but offered little in the way of privacy.

The use of a small, light wash- or nightstand in the country cottage became common at the turn of the nineteenth century, and many would have been mass-produced with simple turned legs. However, even in a modern house setting there is still a place for this type of furniture, particularly if the 1/12 scale occupant has a matching china bowl and jug set.

There are many variations of this piece of furniture and the miniaturist can choose to make their own version unique. Some washstands had a hole in the table top (placed either centrally or to one side) to hold the bowl of water steady, but many did not and were simply a small, convenient table. Other variations that occurred in more prosperous homes would have included a marble top, a tiled back to the three-sided gallery, a drawer, and possibly a towel rail. The bottom shelf would have been a convenient place either for a slop bucket or, in the case of a nightstand, a chamber pot.

To begin with, this project is made in a very similar way to the breadboard (see page 22). It is then finished off with a framework similar to that used for the table project (see page 42), but with the addition of a lower shelf for a chamber pot.

PROJECT 7

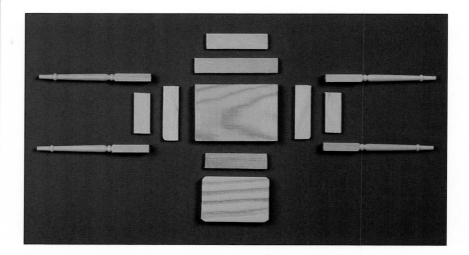

Method

- Saw a piece of strip wood approximately 1⅜in (35mm) by 2in (50mm) for the table top, and sand the edges smooth.

- Measure one of the long edges and saw a section of craft stick (avoiding the rounded ends) to exactly the same length. Again, sand the cut ends lightly.

- To form the back of the stand, glue the piece of craft stick in place on one of the long edges. Use the gluing board to ensure that it forms a right angle.

- Measure the side of the washstand top and cut two more pieces of craft stick to form the sides of the gallery.

- With sandpaper, round off one corner on each of the two sides and smooth the sawn edges.

- Glue them in position so that the top of the stand has three raised

sides, with the rounded corners at the open end.

- Take four spindles, decide on the height of the legs and cut off any excess. I suggest 2⅜in (60mm) long. It is best to reduce the size from the squared-off end, but this will depend on the type of spindle you are using. As always, lightly sand the cut ends and make sure that all four legs are the same size.

- Using craft sticks, cut two pieces 1½in (38mm) and two pieces 1in (25mm). These will form the underframe of the table and, together with the legs, will give the finished piece added strength.

- The base of the washstand is made using the same instructions as the table. Stand the table leg upside down (i.e. with the squared end pointing downwards) in the corner of the

Tools

- Hacksaw or razor saw
- Mitre block
- Sandpaper
- Gluing board
- Metal ruler
- Fine pencil

WASHSTAND

gluing board. Glue one end of a longer frame piece to the leg, making sure that it is aligned with the side of the gluing board. Next take one of the shorter frame pieces and stick it to the same leg, but aligned with the other wall of the gluing board. Once the glue has dried, repeat with the second leg.

- Place the other legs, one at a time, in the corner of the gluing board and complete the building of the base.

- Once it is dry and you have lightly sanded the cut ends, place the table top upside down, so that the underside is uppermost. Lift the support frame and legs (once they are dry) and place glue on the edges that will be stuck to the table. Gently place the legs and frame onto the table, leaving an even space around the edges to act as an overhang.

- Once the glue is dry, carefully measure the size of the space between the legs at the level that you would like the lower shelf to be, and cut a piece of 1⅛in (28mm) strip wood to fit.

- Round off the corners with sandpaper, and stick the shelf in position by gluing the corners to the spindles.

- Once the glue has dried, finish the washstand with paint, wood stain or varnish.

Materials

- Strip wood
- Small craft (or ice-lolly) sticks
- PVA glue

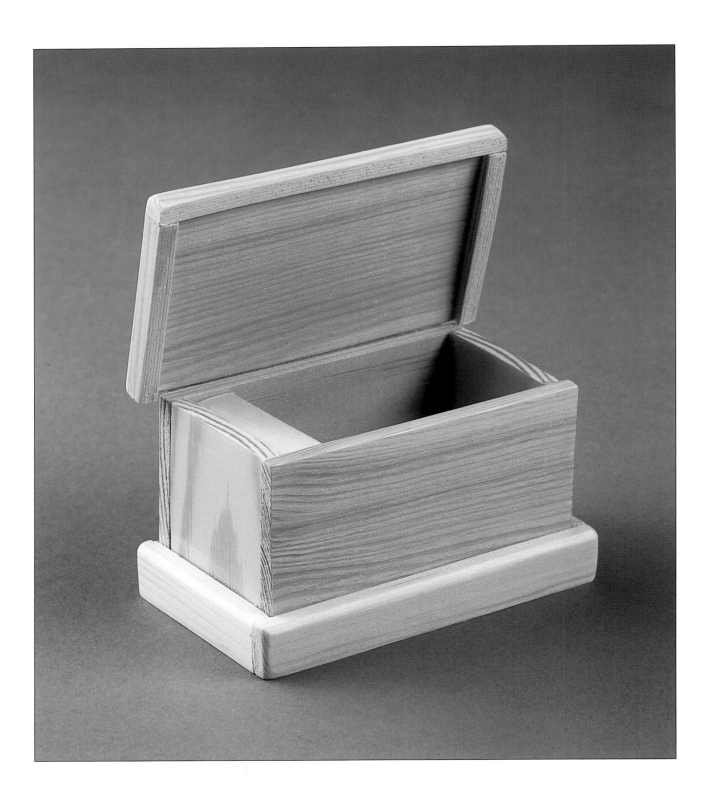

PROJECT 8

Dowry chest

Before wardrobes were in common use, a family would often have kept precious items, as well as their clothes, in a chest. These may have contained smaller boxes, such as a candle box, a removable drawer, or even a set of drawers with access from the outside. They would have been known by various names depending on their use. For instance, in England many were called blanket boxes; in Scotland, a kist. In Ireland they were sometimes referred to as an American chest, which is a reference to the mass migration of Irish people during the potato famine of the mid-nineteenth century. Other types included seamen's boxes, mule boxes and dowry chests.

Dowry chests were the original 'bottom drawer', used by young girls to collect items of clothing and linen in preparation for marriage. Nothing was wasted in the households of yesteryear and, having served its purpose as a dowry chest, the box would then be used as a storage place.

Although they were large items, chests were moved frequently, so they were fitted with handles – rope for a seamen's chest (as salt water would not corrode it), or leather or metal handles. Boxes that were more decorative had bracket feet or a plinth base, and may have been in use in children's rooms or servants' quarters.

The finish on this 1/12 scale box will depend on whether it is used as a piece of furniture or as an heirloom. In the former case, it would be painted. The latter, like the one handed down through my family, would be stripped back to the original wood to reveal the marks of time. Full-size versions often have marks and scratches that bear testament to their past, such as deep parallel scratches that could have been caused by moving them on and off a cart.

PROJECT 8

Method

- Using strip wood, cut three pieces 3in (75mm) by 1¾in (45mm). These will form the back, lid and front of the chest. Then saw two pieces 1⅜in (35mm) by 1¾in (45mm) to form the sides, and lightly sand the sawn edges.

- Using the gluing board to ensure right-angled joints, glue the two side pieces to the back section of the chest.

- Before gluing the front of the chest in place, measure and cut a section to fit the base of the chest from strip wood 1⅜in (35mm) wide. Glue the base in position, using a clamp to hold the sections while waiting for the glue to dry.

DOWRY CHEST

- It will also be easier at this stage to build-in the candle box. Take a craft stick and, avoiding the rounded ends, cut three pieces 1⅜in (35mm) long to form the base, front and lid of the integral candle box (no sides are needed as the chest itself will form these). Lightly sand the cut ends, and glue the base and front together using the gluing board.

- Once it is dry, glue the candle box in position just below the top edges of the chest (remembering to leave enough room for the lid). The front of the dowry chest can now be glued in position.

- Cut off a piece of the cotton tape that is slightly shorter than the candle-box lid and glue it to the lid, with enough left free to use as a hinge. When this is completely dry, stick the lid in place inside the body of the chest so that the candle box can be opened.

- Take the wood that you have cut for the lid of the dowry chest and set it in place, holding it temporarily with sticky tape.

- Using strip wood ½in (13mm) wide, measure and cut two lengths for the plinth to fit the sides of the chest. Once these are glued in position, measure and cut a length for the front plinth (this will be the same size as the front, including the ends of the side plinths, which are already in position).

- Glue the front piece of plinth in position.

- Once the glue has dried, gently round off the top edges and the corners of the plinth.

- Cut a section of ½in (13mm) wide strip wood in half lengthways, and then cut two lengths to form lips for the sides of the lid. Glue these in place, taking care not to glue the chest lid closed.

- Once these two pieces are secure, measure the front edge (including the ends of the side lips) and cut another piece to form the front section of the lip. Glue in position.

- Sand the top outside edge and the corners to round them off.

- With the lid held in place temporarily by sticky tape, attach a piece of cotton tape to the back edge of the lid and the back of the chest itself. This will form the hinge.

- Finish the chest by painting, staining or varnishing.

Materials

- Craft (or ice-lolly) sticks
- Small pieces of cotton tape for the hinges
- PVA glue

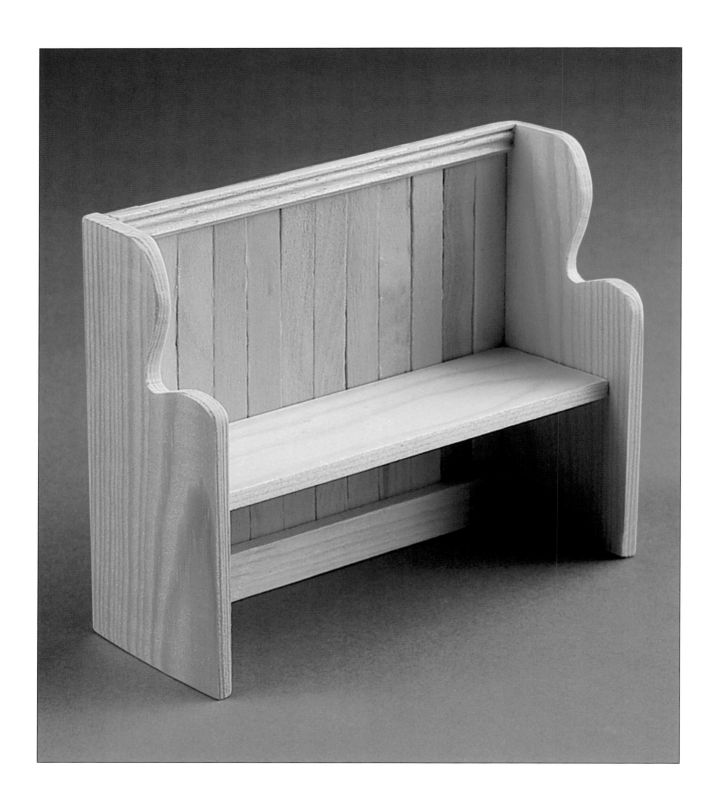

Settle

The settle was originally found in the farmhouses and inns of rural England, before becoming popular throughout the rest of the British Isles. As it moved through the regions it underwent some changes, both in use and design. The incorporation of a box-like structure to house a bed was probably the most major alteration, although this was mainly confined to Ireland.

At its peak, the settle was a common feature in many cottages and houses. Never upholstered, it would have had a high back and side panels to keep out draughts, and would have been placed close to the fire for the adults of the house to sit on. Many would have had a shelf at the top of the back panelling as a means of creating extra storage space. This was often preferable to incorporating storage space or a bed in the seat, as this could make it uncomfortably high.

This version is simply used as a seat, and is relatively straightforward to make. The instructions introduce the use of craft (or ice-lolly) sticks to simulate tongue-and-groove joints. It is one of the larger pieces and should reward the miniaturist with a completed item of some authenticity.

PROJECT 9

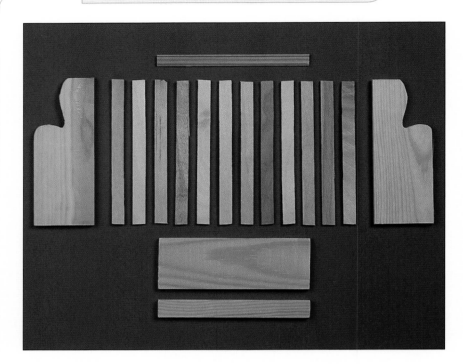

Method

- Take twelve craft sticks, bind them together with sticky tape, and saw off the rounded section at one end. Measure and cut 4in (100mm) from the sawn ends, and then lightly sand both sets of cut edges.

- Using the gluing board, lay down (flat) and glue together all the pieces of craft stick, until they form the tongue-and-groove back of the settle. Use a damp cloth to wipe off any excess glue, and then place a heavy object (such as a tin can) on top until the piece has dried.

- Measure across the 12 sticks, cut a piece of architrave to that length, and glue it in place at the top. Then stick a ½in (13mm) wide piece of strip wood the same length as the architrave to the bottom end of the craft sticks to act as a support.

- Cut the two side pieces from 1⅜in (35mm) wide strip wood. They should be 4in (100mm) in length, and the top ends should be cut into the shape shown in the settle-end template (see page 84) using a fret saw. It is important that both are identical, so they should be taped together before cutting.

- Lightly sand the cut edges.

- With a pencil, lightly mark a line across the side pieces and across the tongue-and-groove back

Tools

- Hacksaw or razor saw
- Mitre block
- Sandpaper
- Gluing board
- Metal ruler
- Fine pencil
- Fret saw
- Fret table or vice
- Tracing paper
- Metal ruler
- Sticky tape
- Tin can

SETTLE

1½in (38 mm) from the base. This shows the height of the seat.

- Place one of the sides on the gluing board, then glue the back of the settle in place. This can be held in place with a weight or sticky tape until the glue is dry.

- Before gluing the other side piece in position, stick the seat section along the pencil line drawn earlier. Hold everything together with clamps while the glue dries, if necessary.

- When the seat has dried, glue the final side section in place.

- Lightly sand any remaining rough edges, and complete with your choice of finishes.

Materials

- Craft (or ice-lolly) sticks
- Strip wood
- Architrave
- PVA glue

Ladder-back chair

Many different styles of chairs evolved over the centuries. Some were made up of a mixture of woods from ancient hedgerows, such as ash and elm. Others were copies of those found in wealthier households. In Ireland, the shape of chairs evolved from stools, with the legs held in position under a thick seat by wedges.

Ladder-back chairs are found in many forms, from the simple version shown here to ones with elaborately turned spindles. Sometimes the stretcher between the two front legs was set high up and used as a place for hanging wet socks in front of the fire. Turned onto its back, another use for a ladder-back chair, when made like this one but without the stretchers, was as a safe place for resting a toddler.

In rural homes, domestic and social life revolved around the fire, which was the only source of heat and perhaps even the only source of light. Eventually the table supplanted the fire as the central feature of the home, although in Ireland the fire still kept its importance. This item of furniture is aimed to provide the dolls' house occupant with a chair that will look equally at home placed at the table or near to the fire, depending on your choice of setting. It combines a number of skills that have been learned in earlier projects in the book.

PROJECT 10

Tools

- Hacksaw or razor saw
- Sandpaper
- Metal ruler
- Fine pencil
- Vice

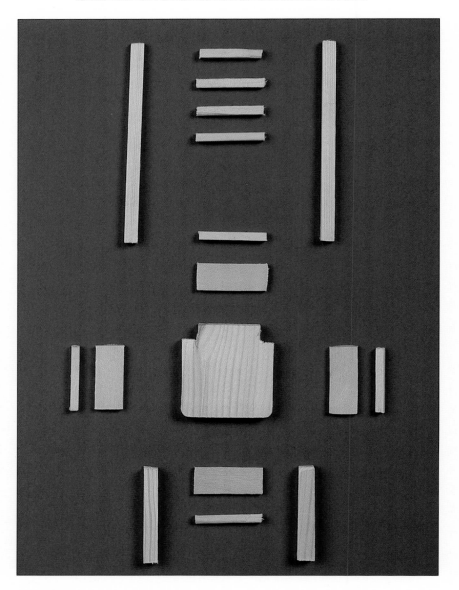

Method

- Take a piece of strip wood 2¾in (70mm) long and ½in (13mm) wide, then cut it carefully lengthways into three equal strips. For safety, secure the wood in a vice if possible.

- Mark a line 1¼in (32mm) from one end on two of the pieces. These will form the back legs of the chair. To form the front legs, take the third strip and cut off two pieces 1¼in (32mm) long.

LADDER-BACK CHAIR

- Cut the seat from a piece of strip wood that is approximately 1¼in (32mm) square. The grain on the finished seat should run from the front to the back.

- Cut the two back corners out of the seat section, as shown in the exploded view, so that the seat will be able to fit around the back uprights.

- At this stage, lightly sand any rough edges using fine-grade sandpaper; smooth all the edges of the seat, and round off the two front corners.

- Using craft sticks, cut two pieces ⅞in (22mm) and one piece ¾in (20mm) long. These will form part of the frame of the chair and, together with the legs, will give the finished piece added strength and stability.

- Again, lightly sand the cut edges as required.

- Using the gluing board to ensure right-angle joints, glue one end of the longer frame piece to the leg. Then take one of the shorter frame pieces and stick it to the same leg, but align it with the other wall of the gluing board. Hold this in place with a weight, clamp or sticky tape until the glue has dried.

- Once dry, repeat the process with the remaining frame piece and the second leg, then glue the two parts together and leave to dry. You should now have a three-sided, open-ended frame with the two front legs glued in place.

- Take the two back legs and glue them to the seat, with the bottom of the seat lining up with the pencil mark.

- Once the glue has dried, turn the seat upside down and glue the leg structure in position.

- Measure the space between the back legs and cut a piece from another craft stick to the correct size. Glue this in place under the seat to complete the frame.

- Measure the space between the back uprights and cut four pieces of matchstick to that length, then glue them in place between the uprights.

- Cut another four pieces of matchstick to make the stretchers, and glue these between the legs. The two side stretchers should be the same height, the back slightly higher, and the front highest of all.

- Sand all the edges to give the chair a worn look. To add detail to the finished piece, wrap some fine sandpaper around a pencil and gently shape the seat to create indentations where legs would cause wear.

Materials

- Strip wood
- Craft (or ice-lolly) sticks
- Matchsticks
- PVA glue

Cradle

No 1/12-scale dwelling would be complete without some reference to the youngest members of the family. In many homes the baby would sleep or play in a cradle placed in the hub of the house – the kitchen. At night, for warmth, he or she was just as likely to be sleeping in the same bed as the parents. Traditionally, the cradle would have been handed down from generation to generation, sometimes having been used for dozens of children.

Some cradles were very plain, some had a modest amount of decoration and some were quite ornate, but there were many features common to all of them. Recycled wood was the norm, and many cradles had rockers made out of sections of cartwheels or wood from a boat that had been shipwrecked or broken up. The latter may have been characterized by marks made by wood-boring insects.

Most cradles had a top or canopy over one end, both to keep the baby out of draughts and to stop unsavoury things falling onto them from the turf or thatch roof. Knobs at the end of the cradle enabled a member of the family to attach a piece of string and to rock the baby to sleep. Some pictures of rural life show a seated woman spinning and rocking the cradle at the same time with a foot.

PROJECT 11

Tools

- Hacksaw or razor saw
- Mitre box
- Sandpaper
- Gluing board
- Metal ruler
- Fine pencil

Method

- Using strip wood that is 1⅜in (35mm) wide, cut three pieces to make the base, head and foot of the cradle. The base section should be 3in (75mm) long, the

head 2in (50mm), and the foot 1in (25mm).

- After sanding any rough edges, stick the head section onto the base, using the gluing board to

CRADLE

form a right-angled join. Once this is dry, repeat with the foot of the cradle.

- Measure the space between the foot and the head of the cradle and, using strip wood that is 1in (25mm) wide, cut two pieces for the sides. Lightly sand the strips and glue them in place.

- Measure and cut two more pieces to form the sides of the cradle hood. Hold these two pieces together with sticky tape and mark a spot at the top, about ¼in (6mm) in from the front edge. Using a ruler, join this mark with the lower front corner of the hood and cut along the line. (The final shape, with its angled front edge, can be seen in the exploded photograph.) Glue them in place after lightly sanding any rough edges.

- Cut a piece of wood that will fit across the top of the hood (covering the tops of side and back pieces).

- Using sandpaper, round off the front edge of the hood top, and glue it in place.

- For the rockers, use ready-made shapes, such as ovals. Stick two or three together to achieve a suitable thickness (if necessary), placing a weight on them while they dry. Mark a line down the centre and cut the shape in half. You will now have two rockers, which can be glued to the underside of the cradle.

- If you are unable to find ready-made ovals, cut two pieces of wood no thicker than a ½in (13mm) to an appropriate length, and, using a tin can or something similar, draw an arc shape. Cut both rockers out together using a fret saw, sand any rough edges, and glue in place.

- Cut a matchstick into two sections that are about ¼in (6mm) longer than the height of the side of the cradle and glue them into the corners, as shown in the photograph.

- Decorate the foot and sides of the cradle using craft sticks (cut in half lengthways) to give a panelled look. This requires accurate measuring, a steady hand and a metal safety ruler to protect fingers, but it does improve the appearance of the finished article.

- Lightly sand, and finish with paint or varnish. The inside of a cradle was generally finished with a cream or other light colour.

Materials

- Strip wood
- Craft (or ice-lolly) sticks
- Curved wood (for the rockers)
- Matchsticks
- PVA glue

PROJECT 12

Chest of drawers

The chest of drawers was popular in a slightly later period than many of the items contained in this book, but could still be made as a cheap and functional piece of furniture. The five-drawer style is fairly typical, with two smaller drawers at the top and three larger ones below as shown here. They had commonly used either bun feet or a plinth, and the latter was sometimes decorated with a cupid's bow. The drawer handles were either turned wood or, in the case of Victorian models, porcelain. If the householder wanted porcelain handles, but was not able to afford them, the wooden handles were simply painted white. As well as period variations, there were also regional contrasts. For example, Scottish versions were frequently taller than their English or Irish counterparts.

This may look like a fairly daunting project, but it uses many of the techniques covered already in earlier projects (the drawers are, in effect, dough-kneading boards with the opening covered by the drawer front). To make the project even easier to follow, the instructions have been divided into three sections.

PROJECT 12

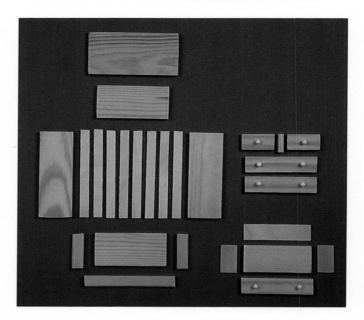

Tools

- Hacksaw or razor saw
- Mitre box
- Sandpaper
- Gluing board
- Craft knife
- Wire cutters

Materials

- Large craft sticks
- Small craft (or ice-lolly) sticks
- Strip wood
- White, spherical map tacks
- PVA glue
- Superglue

Method

Start by cutting the drawer fronts.

- Using ¾in (20mm) strip wood, cut 4 lengths that are 3 inches (75 mm) long. Take one and divide it into 3 additional pieces – 2 equal-sized drawer fronts, and a small central divider.

- Lay all the drawer fronts out on the gluing board in the order that you will see them in the finished piece (i.e. 2 + 1 + 1 + 1). This will help to guide you when arranging the other parts that make up this piece.

- Using 1⅜in (35mm) strip wood, cut 5 equal lengths of wood, making sure that they are marginally longer then the drawer fronts. These will form the dividing shelves, on which the drawers will move in and out.

- You will also need two pieces cut from 1⅜in (35mm) strip wood to make the sides. The correct height of the sides can be established by roughly piecing together the drawers and the dividing shelves. To do this, place the top shelf of the chest of drawers on its side in the corner of the gluing board, then lay the two top drawers in their correct places underneath. (Don't attempt to glue them in at this stage, although sticky tape might help to hold the pieces together.) Put the second shelf in place next, and continue building up the drawers and shelves until the whole chest of drawers is pieced together. Lightly mark the positions of the drawers and the

CHEST OF DRAWERS

shelves, then measure and saw the two side panels to the correct length.

- You should now have a top, three dividing shelves, and a base, as well as two sides for your chest of drawers.

- Place one of the side panels in the corner of the gluing board, and glue the top piece at right angles to it. Once the glue is dry, lay the top two drawer fronts and the divider in position, but do not glue them in place – they should just act as spacers at this stage.

- Glue the next shelf to the side panel (using a try square if necessary to ensure a right-angled join), then glue the divider in place between the top two drawer fronts.

- Continue resting the drawer fronts inside the carcass and gluing the shelves in place, always ensuring that the glue is dry before moving on to the next one. Finally, once the base is in position, glue the second side panel in place.

- As it was unlikely that the back would be seen, often the finish would be quite rough. To reflect this, simply use strip wood, a piece of birch ply or card. For a smarter tongue-and-groove finish, use the same technique as for the settle back.

Now to start work on gluing the drawers.

- Carefully take out the loose drawer fronts that you have been using to guide the position of the shelves, and mark the positions of the drawer handles. Make a start hole with one of the map tacks on each of the drawers, snip the sharp end off using a pair of wire cutters, and glue the map tacks in place with superglue.

- Cut the drawer bases from 1¼in (32mm) strip wood. They should be the same length as the drawers, but ¼in (6mm) shorter than the width of the drawer front.

- Measure one of the long edges of the base and

saw a section of craft stick to exactly the same length (avoiding the rounded ends of the stick). You can use the normal size of craft stick and have a relatively shallow drawer, or the larger size of craft stick and trim it to fit.

- At this stage, lightly sand any rough edges.

- Using the gluing board to ensure a right-angled join, glue the piece of craft stick to the back of the long edge of the drawer base.

- Once the glue has dried, measure the short edges of the drawer (remembering to include the raised back of craft stick that you have already glued to the base), cut two identical side panels from a craft stick and glue them in place.

- Finally, glue the drawer front into position.

- Repeat this for all of the drawers.

Now for the final touches.

- Cut a piece of 1¾in (45mm) strip wood (i.e. strip wood that is marginally wider than the shelves) to form the top surface of the chest of drawers. It should be big enough to leave a small overhang at the sides and front, and be glued in line with the back.

- Once dry, round off the edges of the top piece with a craft knife or sandpaper.

- To make the plinth base, use strip wood that is ½in (13mm) wide. Measure and cut two lengths for the sides, then glue them in position making sure that they are level with the bottom shelf and will not stop the bottom drawer from opening when the front plinth piece is in place.

- Measure and cut a length for the front plinth that is the same size as the front, including the ends of the side plinths. Glue this in place and, once dry, gently round off the top edge and the corners of the plinth.

- Lightly sand the whole piece and finish with paint or varnish.

PROJECT 13

Wall-mounted cupboard

This type of furniture would have been used in a kitchen to offer additional storage, and was popular at a time when living space was at a premium. It would have been useful for displaying prized possessions as well as for everyday use. Many households would have quite a collection of jugs, which were often sold by travelling salesmen as containers filled with jam. These might be displayed either on a wall-mounted cupboard such as this, or on a dresser.

As the focus of family life, and often the only source for heating and cooking in a household, open fires were kept burning for many hours, creating a great deal of soot in the main living area. The sensible housewife would place her plates leaning forwards onto the supporting rail to ensure that as little dust and soot settled on them as possible. In parts of Ireland, bowls placed upside down in a pyramid shape were said to have been 'whamelled'.

PROJECT 13

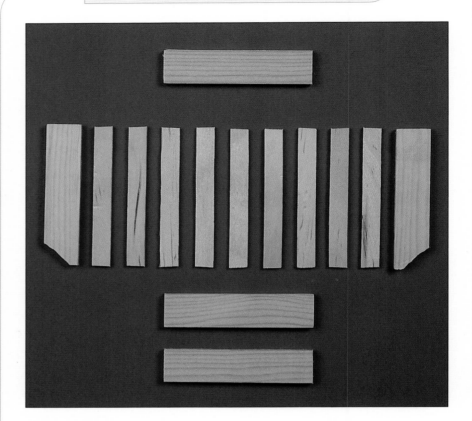

Tools

- Hacksaw or razor saw
- Mitre block
- Fret saw
- Vice or fret saw table
- Sandpaper
- Sticky tape
- Gluing board
- Metal ruler
- Fine pencil
- Needle files
- Tracing paper
- Tin can

Materials

- Strip wood
- Craft (or ice-lolly) sticks
- Ready-made architrave
- Cocktail sticks for plate rails (optional)
- PVA glue

Method

- Bind 9 standard-size craft sticks together with the sticky tape, cut the rounded ends off using a mitre block and hacksaw or razor saw, and then cut a piece 3 inches (75mm) long. Remove the sticky tape and lightly sand the cut ends.

- Using the gluing board to help to keep the angles correct, lay the first piece of craft stick in the corner of the board. Take a second piece and glue very carefully down the long edge. Continue to glue the sticks side by side one at a time, until they

form the tongue-and-groove back of the cupboard.

- Wipe off any spare glue, taking care not to move the tongue-and-groove pieces.

- Once the glue is dry (using a tin can as a weight while the glue dries will ensure that it stays flat), cut two side panels the same length as the back from ¾in (20mm) strip wood.

- Tape the two sides together with sticky tape, trace the template on page 85, and transfer the shape to the bottom of the sides.

WALL-MOUNTED CUPBOARD

Then, with the sides secured in a vice or fretsaw table, cut along the line. Tidy the ends with sandpaper or needle files, until you are happy with the shape.

- Place the back section on the gluing board and, using the side of the board as a guide, glue on the first side panel. Once this is dry, repeat with the other side.

- Measure the width between the two sides and cut four more sections from the strip wood. Glue one in place to form the top, glue another immediately above the shaping on the side panels to make the lower shelf, and finally add the middle shelf.

- Trace the Cupid's bow template on page 84 and transfer it to the fourth piece of strip wood. Holding the wood firmly in a vice or a fretsaw table, cut along the line to make the frieze. Tidy the ends with sandpaper or needle files until you are happy with the shape, and glue in place.

- The next task is to cut and position the architrave around the top edge of the cupboard. Lay the piece of ready-made architrave against the top edge of the cupboard and mark the length of the cupboard top on it.

- To allow the architrave to 'wrap around' the corners of the cupboard, the joins need to be angled (or mitred). To achieve this, place the architrave in a mitre box and, using the angled guides, make a 45° cut at the point of each pencil mark. (The exact position of the mitred joints are shown in the template on page 85.)

- Measure the size of the side architrave sections against the top of the cupboard, and cut angled joints that fit with the front pieces to form a right angle. The back ends of the side pieces only need to be cut straight across, instead of at a 45° angle.

- Stick all three pieces of architrave onto the cupboard, making sure that they create a slight 'lip' above the top.

- Rails can be added to each shelf (as shown in the photograph on page 70) by measuring and cutting two pieces of cocktail stick and placing them into position with a spot of glue.

- The cupboard can be finished with a coat of paint or varnish.

PROJECT 14

Dresser

By definition, fashions tend to come and go, and this is as true for furniture as other areas. However, the dresser has maintained its popularity and can often be found in a modern setting, either as a modern copy or an original.

Dressers were relatively large items that often took up space along a whole wall. Partly because of their size, and often for economy, the dresser was actually built into the fabric of the house as part of a dividing wall. In fact the fitted kitchen probably owes much to the layout of this piece of furniture, with its eye-level storage area, waist-level working surface and low-level cupboards.

It is interesting to note that in a period setting dressers would have distinguishing features depending on the region of origin. The Welsh dresser is probably the one that springs to most people's minds as it was popularized first, but it is not the only example. The use of sledge feet, for instance, originated in Scotland (and later spread to Ireland) as a way of protecting this expensive item of furniture from damp floors.

The Ulster dresser has some unique peculiarities in that the bottom section is frequently uncovered. It was used to house the crocks (large pottery vessels for milk or water), and would be divided into two sections with a 'fiddle' front, or into three sections with the central one being used to house poultry. Today this would be considered a health risk, but a broody goose or hen will not dirty its own nest and would have remained in the central portion of the dresser quite happily. She would only leave the eggs for brief spells in order to go outdoors, and the householder would know that the bird would be safe from any predators until the eggs were hatched.

In other dressers, the lower space was often closed off with small curtains in an attempt to keep the contents of the crocks as clean as possible.

As candles and oil lamps provided only low levels of light, dressers were usually placed opposite the fireplace so that the utensils reflected the light of the flames. As with the wall-mounted cupboard, plates would be tipped forward against a rail to reduce the amount of dust on them, but this also contributed to the reflective effect. Sometimes a strip of leather would have been fixed to the front edge of one of the shelves to hold spoons.

This item is a more complicated piece but it includes elements from several earlier projects, including the dough-kneading board and the wall-mounted cupboard. To make the instructions straightforward they have been divided into three distinct sections – the top part of the dresser, the base, and the drawers.

PROJECT 14

Tools

- Hacksaw or razor saw
- Mitre block
- Fret saw
- Vice or fret saw table
- Sandpaper
- Sticky tape
- Gluing board
- Metal Ruler
- Fine pencil
- Needle files
- Clamps
- Tracing paper
- Tin can

Method

The top section

- Bind 11 standard-size craft sticks together with the sticky tape, cut the rounded ends off using a mitre block and hacksaw or razor saw, and then measure and cut a piece 3 inches (75mm) long, measuring from the cut end. Remove the sticky tape and lightly sand the cut ends.

- Now simply follow the same instructions as the wall-mounted cupboard to create the tongue-and-groove back of the dresser

PROJECT 14

Materials

- Strip wood
- Craft (or ice-lolly) sticks
- Ready-made architrave
- Ready-made coving
- Wooden clothes peg / clothespin
- PVA glue

(see page 71 for the wall-mounted cupboard project).

- Cut two side panels the same length as the back from ¾in (20mm) strip wood.

- Place the back section on the gluing board and, using the side of the board as a guide, glue on the first side panel. Once this is dry, repeat with the other side.

- Measure the width between the two sides and cut three more sections from the strip wood. Glue one in place to form the top, and add another to make the middle shelf.

- Trace the Cupid's bow template on page 84 and transfer it to the third piece of strip wood. Holding the wood firmly in a vice or a fretsaw table, cut along the line to make the frieze. Tidy the ends with sandpaper or needle files, until you are happy with the shape, and glue in place as shown in the photograph on page 74.

- The next task is to cut and position the ready-made architrave around the top edge of the dresser. Once again, simply follow the relevant section of the instructions for the wall-mounted cupboard to achieve this.

The base

- Make a tongue-and-groove back with 11 craft sticks, using the same method as previously.

- Once the back is dry, cut two 3in (75mm) long pieces for the side panels from a 1in (25 mm) wide piece of strip wood.

- Using the gluing board, glue the two sides to the dresser's tongue-and-groove back.

- Measure the distance between the two sides, and cut a further two pieces of strip wood to that length. These will form a base for the bottom section and a shelf for the drawers (this second piece can be put aside for now).

- From 1⅜in (35mm) strip wood, cut a piece that is slightly wider than the bottom section of the dresser, and glue this in place as the top (i.e. the working surface). The edges can be left as they are or rounded off using sandpaper. Also glue in place the base at this stage.

The drawers

- Cut a piece of ⅝in (15mm) strip wood to the same length as the base. This will be used to form the drawer fronts.

- To make false drawers, cut two pieces from a craft stick and glue them onto the piece of strip wood set aside for the drawer fronts. Use two of the leftover round ends from a craft stick to make handles, glue the whole drawer section to the front of the dresser below the work surface, and finally glue the drawer shelf in position.

DRESSER

- To make opening drawers, take the piece for the drawer fronts and place it inside the dresser, against the tongue-and-groove back underneath the work surface. Draw a line along the bottom of the drawer fronts and use a try square to extend this along the side panels. Glue the shelf base in place so that it is immediately below the line.

- Mark a band approximately ½in (13mm) wide on the piece that will be used for drawer fronts. This will be the dividing section between the two drawers.

- Carefully saw the drawer front into three pieces: the left-hand drawer, the central divider and the right-hand drawer. The sawing process in itself will reduce the size of each section by a minute amount, enough to allow the drawers to open freely.

- Glue the divider in position between the work surface and the shelf base.

- The instructions for making the drawers themselves are the same as those used in the chest of drawers project (see page 66). Remember to adjust the sizes as necessary to fit the dresser.

- If the drawers are too tight, sand them until they move more freely. Alternatively, an old trick is to rub candle wax on the wood – if it works for a full-size drawer, it should work for a miniature one.

- When both the top and the base of the dresser are completed and the glue is dry, glue the top of the dresser in place on the work surface. A length of very narrow coving will improve the appearance of the dresser if it is used to cover the tongue-and-groove joints where the top section meets the base (as shown in the photograph of the complete piece).

- Finally, a wooden clothes peg (the type with a spring), carefully taken apart and cut down to the right size, makes ideal 'sledge' feet for the dresser.

- Lightly sand the piece, and finish with your choice of either varnish or paint.

PROJECT 15

Bed

To make an accurate period reproduction, the miniaturist will need to remember that double beds used to be only around four feet wide and shorter than the ones we have today, and will need to adjust the size of their bed according to its age and setting. Although smaller, they would have been much higher than the beds that we are used to, with the space underneath used for storage. Mattresses were made of plaited straw and, later, horsehair.

Many beds were closed in some way to provide both privacy and warmth. Another way to preserve heat was to build the bed into the fabric of the house within an alcove. This also helped to hold up elaborate canopies and curtains.

Beds were (and are) a very large and heavy item of furniture, and would probably have been built *in situ* so that they would not have to be moved.

PROJECT 15

Tools

- Hacksaw or razor saw
- Mitre box
- Sandpaper
- Gluing board
- Metal ruler
- Fine pencil
- Craft knife
- Vice

BED

Method

- To make the head- and footboards cut two pieces 3½in (88mm) long from strip wood that is approximately 1¾in (45mm) wide. Measure and lightly mark the centre of one of the long ends, then make two marks ¾in (20mm) down from the top edge on the shorter sides. Join the marks to make an upturned V, tape the two pieces together, and saw along the line. Finally, lightly sand the edges.

- From ¼in square (6 x 6mm) strip wood, cut six pieces 3½in (88mm) long to make the ends of the frame and the legs, and two pieces 5¾in (145mm) long for the sides of the frame.

- Lightly mark a point 1¼in (32mm) from the bottom (i.e. the floor end) of the four leg pieces.

- Place one leg in the corner of the gluing board and glue one of the end pieces of the frame to it at the point of the pencil mark.

- Glue the headboard in place on the end piece of the frame.

- To complete the head end of the bed, add the second leg, again using the gluing board. As both ends are identical, repeat the processes to make the foot end. (There will be a small ledge on one side of both end pieces,

which should be on the outside of the completed bed.)

- To complete the bed's main structure, glue the side pieces in place at the same height as the end pieces. The bed should now be taking shape and able to stand alone.

- Bind 9 standard-size craft sticks together with the sticky tape, cut the rounded ends off using a mitre block and hacksaw or razor saw, and then cut again to leave 4in (100mm) lengths. Remove the sticky tape and lightly sand the cut ends.

- Take three of the sticks, glue one in the centre of the base frame and the other two pressed up against the end boards, one at each end.

- When these are dry, fill the gaps with the remaining sticks glued at regular intervals.

- For added authenticity, use a craft knife to cut narrow segments from a cocktail stick and glue two on each bedpost, as shown in the photograph on page 80. These simulate the round heads of the bolts that would hold the frame of a full-size bed together.

- Lightly sand, and finish in your choice of varnish or paint.

Materials

- Strip wood
- Craft (or ice-lolly) sticks
- Cocktail stick

TEMPLATES

Patterns for decoration

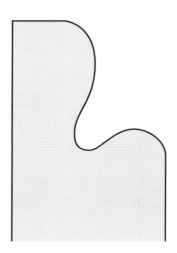

Settle end

Cupid's bow

Side of wall-mounted cupboard

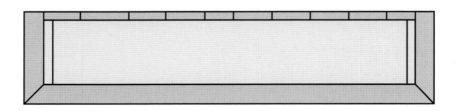

Top of wall-mounted cupboard (showing mitre joints)

GLOSSARY

Apron
A frame around the underside of a table top, to which the top and legs are fastened

Architrave
Moulding, usually around a door or window

Bracket
A shaped support attached to, and projecting from, the body of an item

Bun feet
Flattened versions of ball or rounded feet

Butt joint
A joint where the edges of two boards are against each other and do not overlap or interlock

Carcass
The box-like framework of an item of furniture

Chamfer
To cut off the edge or corner (usually at a 45° angle)

Clingfilm
A thin, clear polythene material, normally used to cover food

Coving
A concave moulding

Fascia
A long, flat surface on the upper part of a piece of furniture

Frieze
A decorative horizontal band

Gallery
A decorative upright trimming or moulding along the top of a table, tray or shelf.

Grain
The appearance, size and direction of the alignment of the fibres in wood

MDF
Medium-density fibreboard

Mitre box
An apparatus designed to guide a saw while cutting mitre joints

Mitre joint
The joint between two pieces of wood that forms a 90° angle with the line of the junction bisecting the angle

Newel post
A post at the top or bottom of a flight of stairs that supports a handrail

Patina
The finish that usually results from wear or usage

Plinth
A block upon which the mouldings of trim are placed, or the base or lower parts of a piece of furniture

PVA
Polyvinyl acetate – glue that dries clear and sets relatively quickly

Set square
An instrument with two arms set at 90 degrees from each other, used to lay out or measure right angles

Spindle
A turned decorative piece, such as a baluster or table leg

Stretcher
A timber rod used especially when horizontal as a tie or brace in framed work, such as a rod or bar extending between two legs of a chair or table

Tongue-and-groove joint
A joint made by a tongue on one edge of a board fitting into a corresponding groove on the edge of another board

Try square
An instrument used for laying out or measuring right angles, usually with a metal blade fixed at 90 degrees from a wooden handle

Turned
Symmetrically shaped or rounded wood

Vernacular furniture
Everyday furniture associated with a particular country

Wedge-and-pegged tenon joint
A type of joint secured by pegs or dowels and not glued

USEFUL ADDRESSES

Tools

Tools suitable for the miniaturist are becoming more and more widely available. It is worthwhile checking with your local supplier, especially as several well-known makes of electrical tools are introducing hobby drills to their range. Some of the more specialized items, such as miniature try squares, are often obtainable by mail order. I have included some addresses of firms that, at the time of writing, have a catalogue available.

Axminster Power Tool Centre
Axminster, Devon EX13 5HU
Email: exportsales@axminster.co.uk
Website: www.axminster.co.uk
A wide range of power and hand tools; has international mail order

Craft Supplies Ltd
The Mill, Millers Dale, Nr. Buxton
Derbyshire SK17 8SN
Email: sales@craft-supplies.co.uk
Website: www.craft-supplies.co.uk
A wide range of power and hand tools; has international mail order

Hobbies
34-36, Swaffham Road, Dereham
Norfolk NR19 2QZ
Email: enquire@hobbies-dereham.co.uk
Website: www.woodenmodels.com
A wide range of power and hand tools; has international mail order

W. Hobby Ltd
Knight's Hill Square, London SE27 0HH
Email: mail@hobby.uk.com
Website: www.hobby.uk.com
A wide range of power and hand tools; has international mail order

Squires Model and Craft Tools
100 London Road, Bognor Regis
West Sussex PO21 1DD
Email: sales@squirestools.com
Website: www.squirestools.com
A wide range of power and hand tools; has international mail order

Craft Supplies

No list of craft supplies can be definitive, but I have tried to compile a list of places where craft supplies, strip wood and ready-made turned or routed supplies, such as architrave and spindles, can be sourced. Most of them do have websites, will accept international orders, and at the time of writing were located at the addresses shown.

If you have access to the Internet there are many websites containing a huge range of suppliers, artisans and other miniature links throughout the world. *Imagination Mall* (www.imaginationmall.com) is one that I find very useful.

Dennis Nixon
Twigfolly, Attleborough Road
Great Ellingham
Attleborough
Norfolk NR17 1LQ
A good supplier of strip wood

Monkey Puzzle Cottage
53 Woodmansterne Lane, Wallington
Surrey SM6 0SW
A good supplier of strip wood

Craft-Club
Avalon Court, Star Road
Partridge Green
West Sussex RH13 8RY

Borcraft Miniatures
Woodland, Bewholme Road
Atwick, Nr Driffield, Yorkshire YO25 8DP
Email: enquiries@borcraft-miniatures.co.uk
Website: www.borcraft-miniatures.co.uk
Suppliers of mouldings and strip wood

Dijon Ltd
The Old Printworks, Streatfield Road
Heathfield, East Sussex TN21 8LA
Email: info@dijon.co.uk
Website: www.dijon.co.uk
Suppliers of spindles and architrave

The Dolls House Emporium
High Holborn Road, Ripley, Derbyshire DE5 3YD
Email: info@dollshouse.com
Website: www.dollshouse.com
Suppliers of spindles, newel posts

Hatton Woods
Plummery Square, Poundbury Village
Dorchester, Dorset DT1 3GN
Website: www.hattonwoods.com
Suppliers of spindles, newel posts and architrave

Hobbies
34-36 Swaffham Road, Dereham, Norfolk NR19 2QZ
Email: enquire@hobbies-dereham.co.uk
Website: www.woodenmodels.com
Suppliers of strip wood, mouldings and craft supplies

W. Hobby Ltd
Knight's Hill Square
London SE27 0HH
Email: mail@hobby.uk.com
Website: www.hobby.uk.com
Suppliers of strip wood, mouldings and craft supplies

Maple Street
Royston
Hertfordshire SG8 0AB
Email: info@maplestreet.co.uk
Website: www.maplestreet.co.uk
Suppliers of mouldings, spindles, newel posts and craft supplies

Pandoro
Westway House, Transport Avenue
Brentford, Middlesex TW8 9HF
Suppliers of mouldings, spindles and craft supplies

FURTHER READING

Books

I feel that you can never have enough books about things that interest you. Those listed here give you some more ideas for adding to your cottage and creating a rural setting.

Dolls' House Accessories, Fixtures and Fittings
by Andrea Barham
(Guild of Master Craftsman Publications Ltd, 1998)

Dolls' House Furniture: Easy-to-make Projects in 1/12 Scale
by Freida Gray
(Guild of Master Craftsman Publications Ltd, 2002)

Dolls' House Needlecrafts
by Venus Dodge
(David and Charles, 1995)

Dolls' House Soft Furnishings in 1/12 Scale
by Nick and Esther Forder
(David and Charles, 2001)

Easy to Make Dolls' House Accessories
by Andrea Barham
(Guild of Master Craftsman Publications Ltd, 1995)

Irish Country Furniture 1700 – 1950
by Claudia Kinmouth
(Yale University Press, 1993)

Making Miniatures in 1/12 Scale
by Venus and Martin Dodge
(David and Charles, 1989)

Making Period Dolls' House Accessories
by Andrea Barham
(Guild of Master Craftsman Publications Ltd, 1996)

Miller's Pine and Country Furniture Buyer's Guide
by Leslie Graham
(Miller's Publications Ltd, 2001)

The New Dolls' House Do-it-yourself Book
by Venus and Martin Dodge
(David and Charles, 1997)

Periodicals

United Kingdom

Dolls' House Magazine
GMC Publications Ltd
166 High Street, Lewes
East Sussex BN7 1XU

Dolls' House and Miniature Scene
West Street, Bourne
Lincolnshire PE10 9PH
Website: www.dollshousemag.co.uk

Dolls' House World
Avalon Court, Star Road
Partridge Green
West Sussex RH13 8RY
Website: www.dollshouseworld.com

United States

Dollhouse Miniatures
Kalmbach Miniatures Inc
21027 Crossroads Circle
PO Box 1612
Waukesha, WI 53187

Miniature Collector
Scott Publications
30595 Eight Mile
Livonia, MI 48152-1798

Wise Owl Magazines
1926 S Pacific Coast Highway, Suite 204
Redondo Beach, CA 90277
E-mail wiseowl@sprintmail.com

Dolls' House World
Heritage Press, State Line Road
North Bend, OH 45052

Dolls in Miniature
Diversion Publishing Company
Box 411, 30799 Pinetree Road
Cleveland, OH 44124-9939

Small Talk Miniature Newsletter
Small Talk, 289 Walnut Street
Ormond Beach, FL 32174

Australia

The Australian Miniaturist
PO Box 467, Carlingford, NSW 2118

BIBLIOGRAPHY

A Collector's Guide to Popular Antiques in Colour
(Library Books, 1993)

Collecting for Pleasure – Town and Country Kitchens
by Tony Curtis (Bracken Books, 1992)

Collecting for Tomorrow – Kitchenware
by Jo Marshall (BPC Publishers Ltd, 1976)

Irish Country Furniture
by Nicholas Loughnan (Eason and Son Ltd, 1984)

Irish Country Furniture 1700 – 1950
by Claudia Kinmouth (Yale University Press, 1993)

Miller's Pine and Country Furniture Buyer's Guide
by Jo Wood (Miller's Publications Ltd, 1995)

Pine Furniture
by Constance King (Magna Books, 1992)

Traditional Country Style
by Elizabeth Wilhide (BCA, 1991)

ABOUT THE AUTHOR

Alison White, a first-time author with more than thirty years of experience in the health service, lives in Northern Ireland. She is a miniatures enthusiast of long standing, and has been a keen collector of antique country furniture since 1980. Her interest in country antique furniture grew as she collected for her own home, all the while knowing that similar furniture was to be found on display in rural museums such as the Ulster American Folk Park and Arthur Cottage, home to the father of Chester A. Arthur (21st President of America, 1881–85). Now, a new dimension has been added to her interest by being able to reproduce them in 1/12 scale, which allows them to be shared with miniaturists around the world.

INDEX

TITLES AVAILABLE FROM
GMC PUBLICATIONS

BOOKS

Woodcarving

Beginning Woodcarving ....*GMC Publications*
Carving Architectural Detail in Wood:
   The Classical Tradition ....*Frederick Wilbur*
Carving Birds & Beasts ....*GMC Publications*
Carving the Human Figure:
   Studies in Wood and Stone ....*Dick Onians*
Carving Nature:
   Wildlife Studies in Wood ....*Frank Fox-Wilson*
Carving on Turning...*Chris Pye*
Celtic Carved Lovespoons:
   30 Patterns ....*Sharon Littley & Clive Griffin*
Decorative Woodcarving
   (New Edition) ....*Jeremy Williams*
Elements of Woodcarving...................................*Chris Pye*
Essential Woodcarving Techniques ....*Dick Onians*
Lettercarving in Wood: A Practical Course ....*Chris Pye*
Relief Carving in Wood:
   A Practical Introduction ....*Chris Pye*
Woodcarving for Beginners ....*GMC Publications*
Woodcarving Tools, Materials & Equipment
   (New Edition in 2 vols.) ....*Chris Pye*

Woodturning

Bowl Turning Techniques Masterclass ....*Tony Boase*
Chris Child's Projects for Woodturners ....*Chris Child*
Contemporary Turned Wood:
   New Perspectives in a Rich Tradition....................*Ray Leier,*
      Jan Peters &
      Kevin Wallace
Decorating Turned Wood:
   The Maker's Eye ....*Liz & Michael O'Donnell*
Green Woodwork ....*Mike Abbott*
Intermediate Woodturning Projects..........*GMC Publications*
Keith Rowley's Woodturning Projects ....*Keith Rowley*

Making Screw Threads in Wood.........................*Fred Holder*
Turned Boxes: 50 Designs ....*Chris Stott*
Turning Green Wood.............................*Michael O'Donnell*
Turning Pens and Pencils..........................*Kip Christensen &*
      Rex Burningham
Woodturning: A Foundation Course
   (New Edition)...*Keith Rowley*
Woodturning: A Fresh Approach ....*Robert Chapman*
Woodturning: An Individual Approach............*Dave Regester*
Woodturning: A Source Book of Shapes ....*John Hunnex*
Woodturning Masterclass...................................*Tony Boase*
Woodturning Techniques ....*GMC Publications*

Woodworking

Beginning Picture Marquetry ....*Lawrence Threadgold*
Celtic Carved Lovespoons:
   30 Patterns ....*Sharon Littley & Clive Griffin*
Celtic Woodcraft...*Glenda Bennett*
Complete Woodfinishing (Revised Edition) ....*Ian Hosker*
David Charlesworth's Furniture-Making
   Techniques ....*David Charlesworth*
David Charlesworth's Furniture-Making
   Techniques – Volume 2 ....*David Charlesworth*
Furniture-Making Projects for
   the Wood Craftsman ....*GMC Publications*
Furniture-Making Techniques for
   the Wood Craftsman ....*GMC Publications*
Furniture Projects with the Router........................*Kevin Ley*
Furniture Restoration
   (Practical Crafts) ....*Kevin Jan Bonner*
Furniture Restoration:
   A Professional at Work ....*John Lloyd*
Furniture Restoration and
   Repair for Beginners................................*Kevin Jan Bonner*
Furniture Restoration Workshop................*Kevin Jan Bonner*
Green Woodwork ....*Mike Abbott*

Upholstery

Toymaking

Dolls' Houses and Miniatures

Crafts

Gardening

Photography

Art Techniques

VIDEOS

MAGAZINES

The above represents a full list of all titles currently published or scheduled to be published.
All are available direct from the Publishers or through bookshops, newsagents and specialist retailers.
To place an order, or to obtain a complete catalogue, contact:

GMC Publications,
Castle Place, 166 High Street, Lewes, East Sussex BN7 1XU, United Kingdom
Tel: 01273 488005 Fax: 01273 402866
E-mail: pubs@thegmcgroup.com

Orders by credit card are accepted

DISCARD

DISCARD